D1455550

Marie Curie:

Pioneering Physicist

by Elizabeth R. Cregan

MISSION: SCIENCE

Science Contributor
Sally Ride Science

Science Consultant
Jane Weir, Physicist

MISSION: SCIENCE

Sally Ride Science™ is an innovative content company dedicated to fueling young people's interests in science.

Our publications and programs provide opportunities for students and teachers to explore the captivating world of science—from astrobiology to zoology.

We bring science to life and show young people that science is creative, collaborative, fascinating, and fun.

To learn more, visit www.SallyRideScience.com

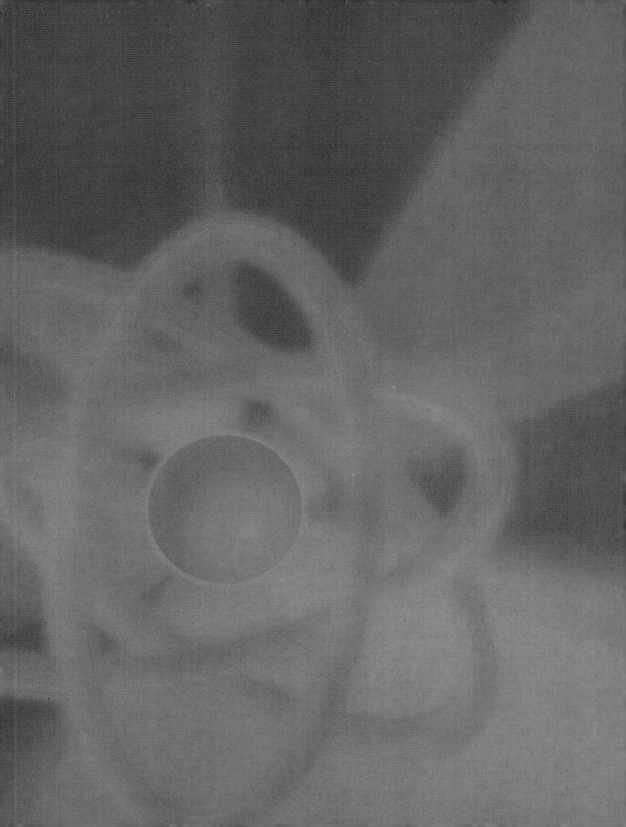

First hardcover edition published in 2009 by
Compass Point Books
151 Good Counsel Drive
P.O. Box 669
Mankato, MN 56002-0669

Editor: Mari Bolte
Designer: Heidi Thompson
Editorial Contributor: Sue Vander Hook

Art Director: LuAnn Ascheman-Adams
Creative Director: Keith Griffin
Editorial Director: Nick Healy
Managing Editor: Catherine Neitge

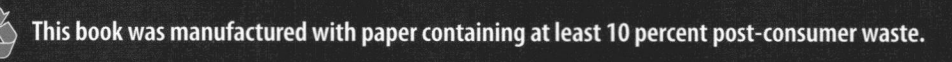 This book was manufactured with paper containing at least 10 percent post-consumer waste.

Library of Congress Cataloging-in-Publication Data
Cregan, Elizabeth R.
 Marie Curie : pioneering physicist / by Elizabeth R. Cregan.
   p. cm. — (Mission: Science)
 Includes index.
 ISBN 978-0-7565-3960-3 (library binding)
1. Curie, Marie, 1867–1934—Juvenile literature. 2. Chemists—Poland—Biography—Juvenile
literature. 3. Women chemists—Poland—Biography—Juvenile literature. I. Title. II. Series.
 QD22.C8C74 2008
 540.92—dc22
 [B]   2008007727

Visit Compass Point Books on the Internet at *www.compasspointbooks.com*
or e-mail your request to *custserv@compasspointbooks.com*

Table of Contents

In 1914, scientist Marie Curie boarded a train in Paris, France. Her destination was Bordeaux, a French city about 350 miles (560 kilometers) away. Curie was barely able to carry the 44-pound (20-kilogram) lead container she brought with her. But the contents had to be taken out of Paris. World War I had just begun, and the German army was about to invade the capital of France. Curie's important cargo was radium, a radioactive element she had discovered in 1902.

The day after arriving in Bordeaux, Curie deposited the radium in a bank vault and returned home. When the war was over in 1918, she brought the radium back to Paris.

Marie Curie is one of the most significant scientists of all time. She spent most of her life studying

Marie Curie spent countless hours in her lab working with radioactive materials.

Radioactivity

Whenever something gives off energy, it produces radiation. For example, the sun radiates heat and light. Marie Curie did not think radiation was the right word to describe the energy coming from the substances she studied. She named this energy radioactivity. Today we know that radioactive substances give off energy when the nuclei of their atoms break down.

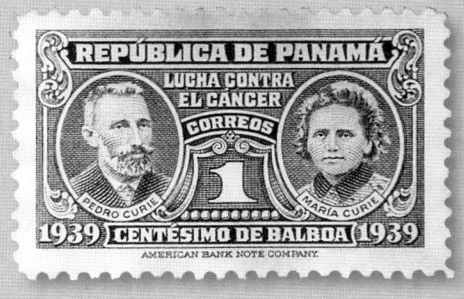

radioactivity, a word she created to describe energy given off by elements. Her pioneering research focused on radium and polonium, the two elements she and her husband, Pierre, had found during their research.

In 1902, Marie and Pierre Curie received the world's highest award for science—the Nobel Prize in physics. Marie was the first woman to win the award. Her work was so successful that she won a second Nobel Prize in chemistry in 1911.

Curie was known as a brilliant scientist and a hard worker. She experimented tirelessly until she found answers to her questions. Her studies helped other scientists understand how atoms work. Her research helped others find new ways to treat cancer. However, her work was also dangerous. She eventually died from the effects of radioactivity.

The Nobel Prize

The first Nobel Prize was awarded in 1901. It is given each year to men and women for their work in physics, chemistry, literature, physiology or medicine, and peace. The winners receive a medal, a diploma, and money to continue their work.

As of 2007, 777 individuals and 20 organizations had been awarded the Nobel Prize. Only 34 of these were women. Besides the Curies, three other married couples share a Nobel Prize—and one of the couples is the Curies' daughter, Irène, and her husband, Frédéric Joliot.

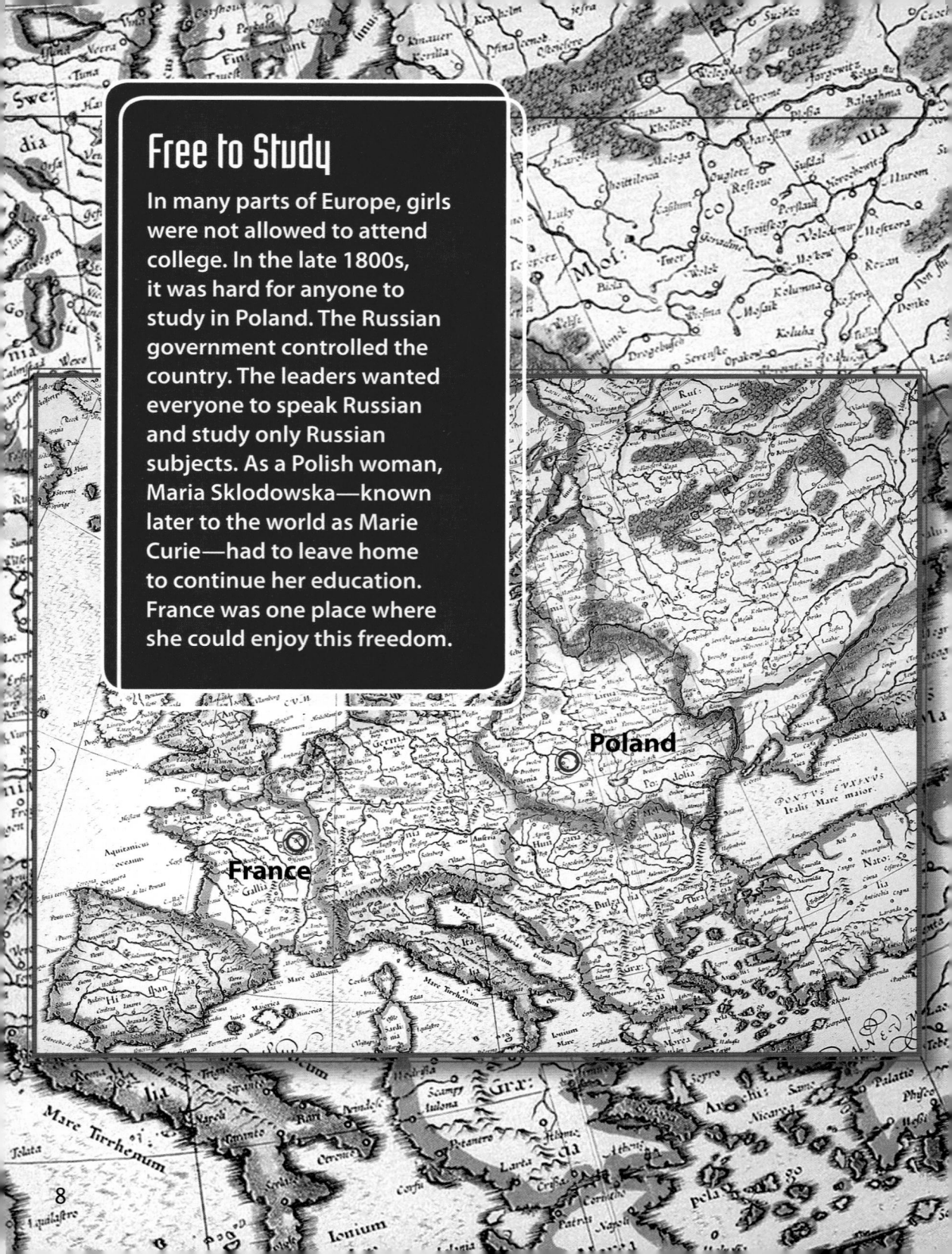

Free to Study

In many parts of Europe, girls were not allowed to attend college. In the late 1800s, it was hard for anyone to study in Poland. The Russian government controlled the country. The leaders wanted everyone to speak Russian and study only Russian subjects. As a Polish woman, Maria Sklodowska—known later to the world as Marie Curie—had to leave home to continue her education. France was one place where she could enjoy this freedom.

Poland

France

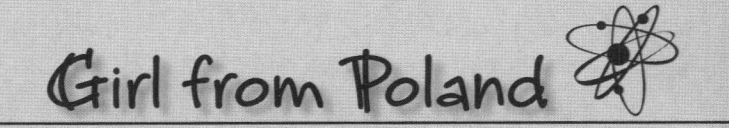

Marie Curie was born Maria Sklodowska on November 7, 1867, in Warsaw, Poland. Her father was a high school science teacher, and her mother was the principal of a private school for girls.

Maria's favorite school subjects were science and language arts. She was an exceptional student and graduated from high school at the age of 15. Although she wanted a college education, Polish girls were not allowed to attend a university. Going to school in another country was out of the question since it was too costly for her parents.

Maria and her older sister, Bronia, came to an agreement. Maria would work as a tutor to help pay for Bronia to go to medical school. Once Bronia received her medical degree, she would help pay for Maria's education. The plan worked. Bronia attended the Sorbonne, also known as the University of Paris. When she graduated and became a doctor, Maria enrolled at the Sorbonne in 1891. She was 24 years old.

Maria Sklodowska (left) with her father and two sisters, Helena and Bronia. She also had a brother, Josef, and another sister, Sofia, who died from typhus in 1876.

9

To earn money for the future, Marie took a job as a governess, teaching children of a Polish family.

To fit in better at the Sorbonne, Maria adopted the French spelling of her name—Marie. While at school, she lived alone in a small, drafty attic. But she was glad just to be able to study. Classes were taught in French, and Marie could only speak Polish. But she quickly learned to read, write, and speak French. She wouldn't let anything stop her from getting an education.

Marie initially had some trouble with math. She hired a math tutor and worked extra hours to conquer her least favorite subject. She enjoyed science classes and devoted herself to courses in chemistry and physics, studying late nearly every night.

Did You Know?

While working as a governess, Marie fell in love with the family's oldest son, and at one point, the couple was even engaged. Her employers did not approve, and eventually the couple went their separate ways.

The Sorbonne, also known as the University of Paris, is Europe's oldest university. Marie would eventually become the Sorbonne's first female professor.

Often Marie studied so intensely that she forgot to eat. But her hard work paid off, and she graduated at the top of her class—and the best in physics. Despite her early troubles with math, she went on to earn a degree in mathematics. She finished second in her class and even won a math scholarship.

Hungry?

Did you know that it took a chemist to make the cereal floating inside your breakfast bowl? Cereal chemists study grains such as wheat, rice, corn, and oats and figure out how to make them into cereals. Since grains are the base of the world's food supply, studying their chemistry is a growing field. Cereal chemists spend most of their time in the lab looking for the best way to make cereal products.

After earning an undergraduate degree from the Sorbonne in 1893 and a graduate degree a year later, Marie was offered a job studying magnets. She studied how they interacted with various kinds of steel. In her search for lab space, she met Pierre Curie, a French physicist. He worked as a teacher and was head of the lab at the School of Industrial Physics and Chemistry in Paris. Pierre was already famous for his work with magnets and crystals.

Did You Know?

During the late 19th century, colleges were beginning to accept women as equals to men. The first women's university in England, Girton College, was founded in 1869. In 1875, only around 3,000 women attended coeducational colleges in the United States. But by 1900, there were close to 20,000 in attendance.

Long cycling trips became the Curies' way to take a break from their challenging research.

Marie with daughters Ève and Irène

A Modern Family

Marie was a very practical, organized woman. She was determined to be a good scientist, and she also wanted to be a good wife and mother. It was important to her and Pierre that they continue their work together. So she hired a servant to do work around the house. She also asked Pierre's father to baby-sit the children.

In July 1895, Marie and Pierre were married in Sceaux, France, Pierre's hometown. The following year, Pierre became a professor at the Sorbonne. Marie was his assistant. The couple would have two daughters, Irène and Ève, in 1897 and 1904.

Society made it difficult at the time for female scientists to work alone. So women like Marie worked as a team with their husbands. Pierre eventually gave up his own research on magnets and turned to Marie's study of elements and radiation.

While Marie conducted her research, she also worked part time as a teacher at a girls' school. At the same time, she was working toward her doctoral degree, the highest college degree a person can earn. As she searched for a subject for her doctoral thesis, she became interested in the work of two scientists. One had discovered X-rays. The other had found that the element uranium gives off rays of energy.

The light in a 1904 drawing of the Curies symbolizes how amazing their discoveries were.

Labs: Then and Now

Marie's laboratory was an old shack with a leaky roof where medical students used to dissect human bodies. Curie sweltered in the summer and froze in the winter. It was impossible to control the conditions in the lab, but it was the only place the Curies could conduct their experiments.

Modern scientists can't imagine how Curie managed to work under such conditions. Modern labs are clean and comfortable. The Institut Curie in Paris, France, which is named after Curie, has some of the best lab conditions available today.

The Curies had a hunch that the energy from uranium had to do with its atoms. Atoms are the basic building blocks that make up everything in the universe. By experimenting with uranium, Curie concluded that energy from an element comes from the atom itself, not how the atoms are arranged.

Marie and Pierre tested other elements to see if they also emitted radiation. Separating the elements and analyzing them was difficult work. They needed large amounts of a costly brownish-black mineral called pitchblende. They found large amounts of it at a mine in Bohemia in what is now the Czech Republic.

They needed more room for their experiments. The principal of the school where Pierre worked offered them a large shed. There they carried out the challenging work of separation and analysis.

Atomic Weight

In the early 1800s, English chemist John Dalton studied atoms. He found that the atomic weight, or the weight of a single atom, was different for each element. The lightest atom, hydrogen, has two hydrogen molecules and an atomic weight of 1.00794. The atomic weight of uranium is 238.0289. Some heavy atoms are uranium, radium, and plutonium.

In the late 1800s, Russian scientist Dimitri Ivanovich Mendeleev grouped elements by their atomic weights. He created what is called the periodic table of the elements. At that time, scientists had discovered 63 elements, but Mendeleev predicted that more would be discovered in the future. He was right. The Curies discovered polonium and radium in 1898. By the end of the 1900s, scientists had discovered more than 110 elements.

Polonium and Radium

Marie's job was separating the elements. She wrote, "Sometimes I had to spend a whole day stirring a boiling mass with a heavy iron rod nearly as big as myself. I would be broken with fatigue at day's end." But her experiments paid off. In June 1898, the Curies discovered a new element. It gave off about 300 times more energy than uranium.

Marie called it polonium, after her native country, Poland. Curie didn't think radiation was the right word to describe the powerful energy that elements such as polonium gave off. So she made up the word *radioactive* to describe this kind of powerful radiation.

About five months later, Marie found another active element. She called it radium. The Curies also determined the atomic weight of each new element.

Marie's doctoral thesis ➡ received great praise. Examiners commented that Marie's paper contributed more to scientific research than any previous thesis project.

THÈSES

PRÉSENTÉES

A LA FACULTÉ DES SCIENCES

POUR OBTENIR

LE GRADE DE DOCTEUR ÈS SCIENCES PH

PAR

Mme SKLODOWSKA CURIE.

1re THÈSE. — RECHERCHES SUR LES SUBSTANCES ACTIVES.

2e THÈSE. — PROPOSITIONS DONNÉES PAR LA FA

Soutenues le juin 1903, devant la Commission d'Ex

MM. LIPPMANN, *Président.*
BOUTY,
MOISSAN, } *Examinateurs.*

A Determined Scientist!

The Curies bought tons of pitchblende in 50-pound (23-kg) bags. Marie dumped nearly 40 of these bags into a large pot and added acid and water. For hours, she stirred the mixture with a long metal rod to help dissolve the pitchblende. The metal rod was nearly as tall as she was. But her experiment was successful, and she ended up with a 10th of a gram of a new element—radium.

Surrounded by Radiation

Radiation is everywhere—in your bedroom, in your classroom, and even in your body. But not all radiation is as strong and dangerous as the energy from radium.

In fact, without the sun's radiation, there would be no life on Earth. But too much of a good thing can be dangerous. Working on your suntan for hours and hours can damage your tissues and lead to illnesses such as skin cancer.

By 1903, Marie finished her doctoral thesis—*Research on Radioactive Substances*. She believed her discovery belonged to the whole world. Both Marie and Pierre openly shared the details of their research with other scientists.

The Effects of Radioactivity

The important research done by Marie and Pierre Curie came at a high price—their health. They began feeling tired all the time. They were losing weight. Their fingers were numb from handling radium. The skin on Marie's fingers became cracked and scarred from working with radioactive materials. Pierre's hands were also scarred, and sometimes his arms and legs shook. Sometimes he had a hard time standing. He had a permanent gray mark on his arm where he had strapped a sample of radium for 52 days.

RIS

The Nobel Prize

In 1903, the Curies were jointly awarded the Nobel Prize in Physics for their research on radiation. Henri Becquerel also shared the award for his discovery of radioactivity. At first, the award was to go to just Pierre and Becquerel. But Pierre refused it unless Marie was included. Marie was the first woman to receive the Nobel Prize. By the time it was presented, the Curies were too sick to travel to Stockholm, Sweden, to accept the award.

The Curies became known all over the world. Newspapers printed articles about their discoveries. They were especially interested in the fragile woman who stirred the huge pot of pitchblende to get a tiny amount of radium. Journalists from all over wanted to interview them. The quiet solitude in which they did their experiments was shattered. Pierre wrote in July 1905, "A whole year has passed since I was able to do any work."

Support For Female Scientists

It has not always been easy for women to have a career in science. Some female scientists believe women have a harder time advancing in the field. Myrtle Hildred Blewett (1911–2004) studied physics all her life. She believed she was held back in her career because she was a woman. Early in her education, she had to stop studying for a while because she didn't have the money to continue. She didn't want that to happen to other women in physics. When she died in 2004, Blewett left almost all her money to the M. Hildred Blewett Scholarship for Women in Physics. The first scholarship was awarded in 2005. She intended that money to be used for women who want to return to physics after taking time off to care for their families.

The Curies realized that radioactivity was killing the cells in their bodies. They also realized that it could kill unhealthy cells. Perhaps it would be useful in treating cancer.

The effects of radioactivity didn't stop the Curies from handling radioactive materials. They may have ignored the dangers to continue their important work. Pierre often carried a sample of radium in his coat pocket to show to his friends. Marie kept a small sample of radium next to her bed. It glowed in the dark.

Notebooks

After so much exposure to radium, Marie's notebooks and papers became radioactive. Today they are on display at the National Library of France in Paris.

In order to view the notebooks, people have to sign an agreement that they will do so at their own risk. These agreements will need to be signed for a long time—it takes 1,620 years for the effects of radium to decrease by half.

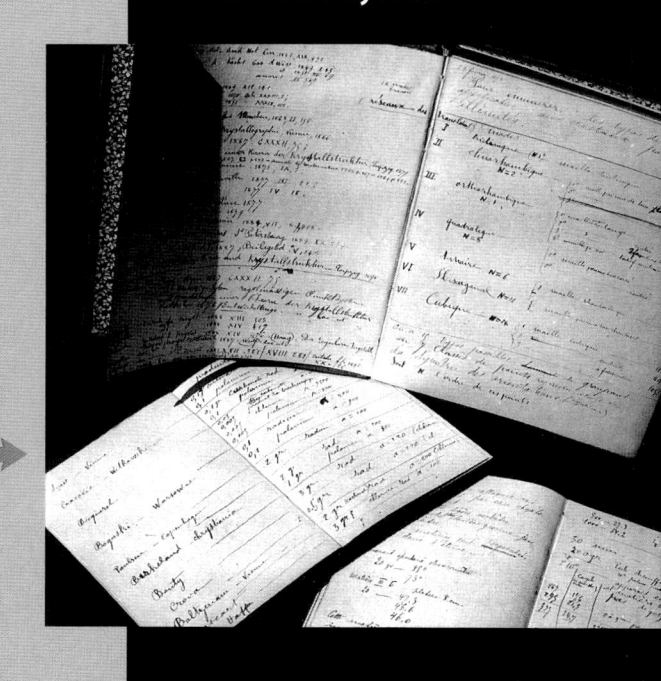

Marie filled several notebooks with notes about her experiments. She also jotted down recipes and how much it cost to have her laundry done.

On a rainy day in April 1906, Pierre Curie rushed through the streets of Paris on his way to a meeting. He stumbled into the path of a horse-drawn wagon and was killed. Just 11 years after their wedding, Marie Curie was left alone to raise their two daughters and continue her research.

In 1908, the Sorbonne asked her to take her husband's position as professor, and she accepted. She became the first female professor in the 650-year history of the university.

Curie continued her research. She studied how to use radium to diagnose and treat diseases. She also wanted to find an exact unit of measure for radiation. This unit of measure is now called the curie unit.

The death of her husband made it difficult for Curie to continue her research and raise her children.

Did You Know?

The curie unit is not the only unit used to measure radioactive samples. There are also becquerels, röntgens, rads, rems, grays, and sieverts.

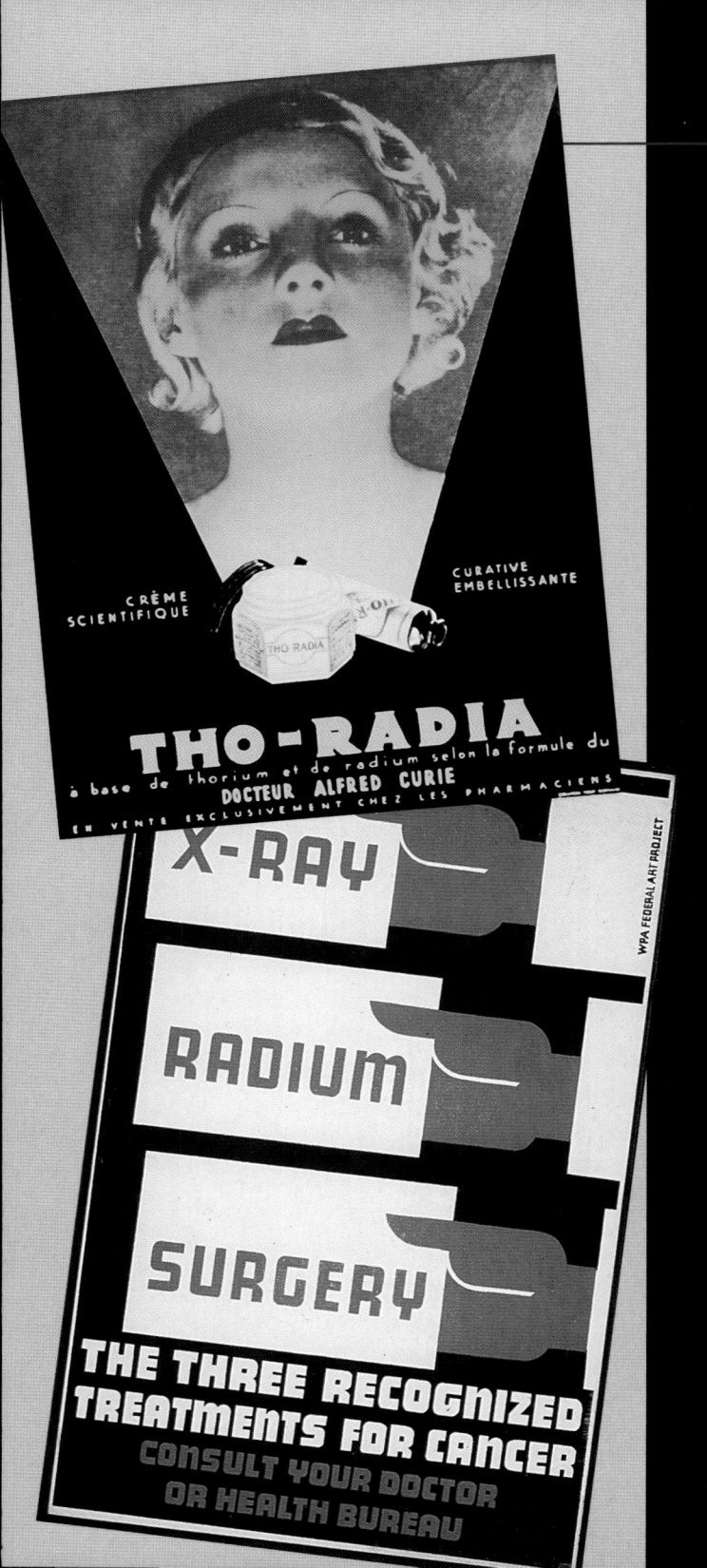

CRÈME SCIENTIFIQUE

CURATIVE EMBELLISSANTE

THO-RADIA
à base de thorium et de radium selon la formule du
DOCTEUR ALFRED CURIE
EN VENTE EXCLUSIVEMENT CHEZ LES PHARMACIENS

WPA FEDERAL ART PROJECT

X-RAY

RADIUM

SURGERY

THE THREE RECOGNIZED TREATMENTS FOR CANCER
CONSULT YOUR DOCTOR OR HEALTH BUREAU

The Radium Craze

Before scientists knew the dangers of radium, people enjoyed using it for all kinds of things. In the early 1900s, people drank it to cure stomach cancer. They added it to paint so watches and airplane instruments would glow in the dark. Makeup included radium, which made it sparkle. Even soap, chocolate bars, and toothpaste contained radium.

Female factory workers who worked with radium were called Radium Girls. The girls noticed that strange things began to happen. When they blew their noses, their handkerchiefs glowed in the dark. Their nails and teeth glowed when they painted them with radium.

People thought radium was safe until the workers began to lose their teeth and die of cancer. By the late 1920s, scientists began to use protection against the harmful radiation.

Radium was now accepted as a new element. The medical community around the world began using it to treat cancer. Curie also discovered an even purer form of radium and found a more accurate atomic weight for the element.

After Pierre's death, Curie never made a new discovery. Some people began to question her abilities. As she continued to handle radium through the years, she got sicker and sicker. Although she was very ill, she continued her work. She still kept detailed records of her research and daily life in her notebooks. She also studied the works of other scientists and agreed with many of their ideas.

In 1911, Curie was awarded a second Nobel Prize. This one was for her contribution to chemistry through her discovery of the elements radium and polonium.

Curie and Einstein

In 1911, Curie attended the first Solvay Conference in Brussels, Belgium. It was the first world conference for physics and chemistry. Albert Einstein was also there. He was the youngest physicist present. The two became friends, and in 1913, Einstein even went on a trip with the Curie family.

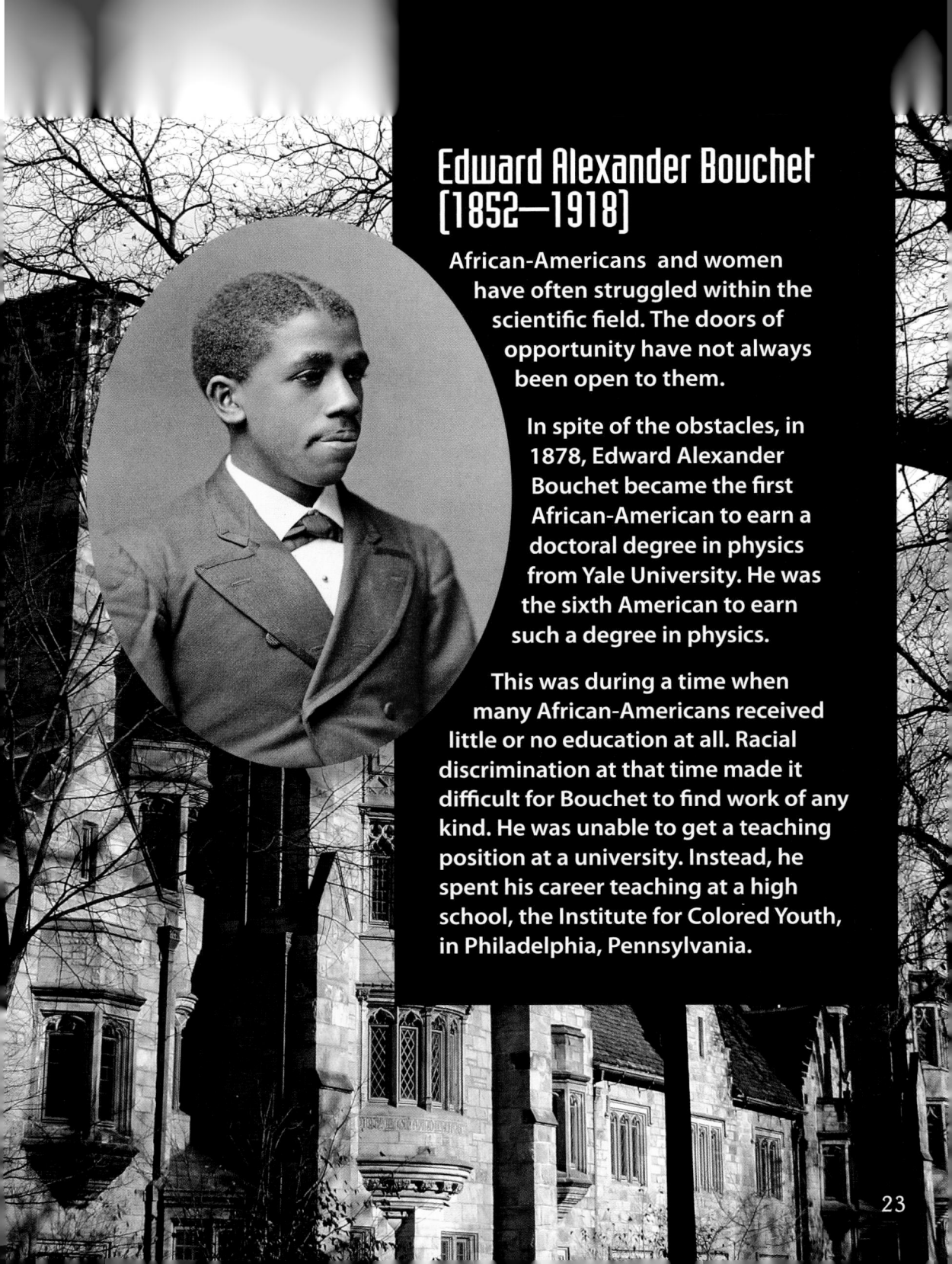

Edward Alexander Bouchet (1852—1918)

African-Americans and women have often struggled within the scientific field. The doors of opportunity have not always been open to them.

In spite of the obstacles, in 1878, Edward Alexander Bouchet became the first African-American to earn a doctoral degree in physics from Yale University. He was the sixth American to earn such a degree in physics.

This was during a time when many African-Americans received little or no education at all. Racial discrimination at that time made it difficult for Bouchet to find work of any kind. He was unable to get a teaching position at a university. Instead, he spent his career teaching at a high school, the Institute for Colored Youth, in Philadelphia, Pennsylvania.

Bringing Her Work to the World

It was always important to Curie that the world benefit from her work. She spent the later part of her life making sure that happened.

Curie was busy planning the Radium Institute, a center for the study of radioactivity, when World War I broke out in 1914. She stopped all work on her project and turned her focus to helping wounded soldiers. It would be another five years before she would open the Radium Institute.

Curie believed that all scientific discoveries should be used to help people. She knew that X-rays were needed to treat injuries and wounds. Doctors would be able to see where bones were broken or where bullets were lodged. So Curie, along with her daughter Irène, worked to make X-ray services available to wounded soldiers. They put X-ray equipment in more than 20 vans that served as mobile hospitals. They also installed about 200 X-ray machines in permanent facilities and trained 150 female volunteers to take X-rays.

Curie also raised funds to buy more X-ray equipment. If there was no one to help load the new equipment and ship it to military hospitals, Curie did it herself. More than 1 million X-rays were taken because of her efforts. However, she and her daughter were exposed to large doses of radiation.

Did You Know?

Today X-rays are used for more than looking at bones. Airports use them to examine luggage and packages for dangerous materials like weapons. Engineers use X-rays to look at metals used for bridges or airplanes and see any cracks or other structural problems. X-rays can even help art collectors know if any changes have been made to paintings.

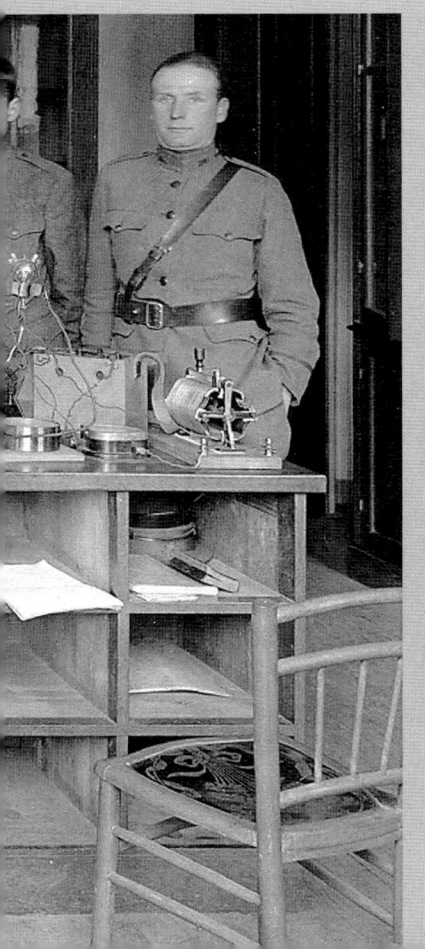

Curie believed that helping soldiers during World War I was more important than her research.

President Warren Harding escorted Curie down the steps of the White House during her visit to the United States of America to receive a donated gram of radium.

Curie finally returned to what she loved to do most—study radium. It was now being used all over the world to treat cancer. This made her famous. It also made radium quite expensive.

At the time, the United States possessed around 50 grams of radium. Curie had only one gram, the one she smuggled out of Paris during the war.

Curie had many admirers in the United States. Ten wealthy American women in particular wanted to help her. They raised more than $100,000 to buy her one more gram of radium.

In 1921, Curie traveled to the United States with her two daughters to accept the generous gift. It was a long, difficult trip since her health was very poor. Her radiation sickness was getting worse.

Curie returned to France with her gift of radium. But she continued to grow weaker and weaker. Her eyesight began to fail, and cancer slowly took over her body. On July 4, 1934, at the age of 66, Marie Curie died. Her death was caused by years of handling radioactive materials.

Curie's work led to many important discoveries. Radiation is still used to treat cancer. It kills organisms that spoil food and produces energy for heat and electricity. It detects smoke in homes and determines the age of dinosaur bones.

Because of Curie, there is a new branch of science—the study of radioactivity. Curie's discovery of radium and its uses changed the way we think about matter and energy. Scientists continue to build on her work.

Curie was often afraid her work would be used to make weapons. The world now knew how dangerous radiation was—it would only be a matter of time before someone found a way to use it for their benefit. Her fears came true more than a decade after her death. In 1945, the atomic bomb was tested in the United States. It was used on Hiroshima and Nagasaki in Japan to end World War II.

But Curie's work also did a lot of good in the world— exactly what she wanted it to do.

Marie (center) continued her search for more radioactive substances until her death. She hired many talented women, favoring those who had been discriminated against in male-dominated laboratories.

Physicist: Shirley Ann Jackson

Rensselaer Polytechnic Institute

Tiny Particles, Big Difference

Shirley Ann Jackson began her career studying tiny particles that are smaller than atoms. Then she studied the physics of electronics and lasers. She earned her Ph.D. from the Massachusetts Institute of Technology in 1973, becoming the first female African-American to earn a doctorate from the school and the second to earn a Ph.D. in physics in the United States. In the 1990s, Jackson found a new way to use her physics know-how. President Bill Clinton asked her to be in charge of keeping nuclear energy safe. In 1999, she became the president of the oldest technological university in the country—Rensselaer Polytechnic Institute.

What has Jackson gained from her past experiences? "In all of those things, it requires an ability to look at complicated things and manage and understand them," Jackson says. "That's the kind of background that one gets doing physics."

Being There

Jackson wanted to study engineering, until she took a college physics class. She now studies the subatomic particles that are found inside atoms. She says, "For me, the world has always been full of mysteries. Studying the physical properties of matter allows me to unlock the secrets of the physical world."

On The Job

Shirley Ann Jackson always loved math. "Math is really fun by itself, but it's also a tool for understanding how things work," she says. Has math helped you understand how something works?

Think About It

Jackson has fought many stereotypes and accomplished many firsts. Have you been the first person to do anything?

Lasers are used to read CDs and DVDs, to cut steel and other metals, and for some surgical procedures.

Jackson has taught both undergraduate and graduate students at Rutgers University.

Life and Work At a Glance

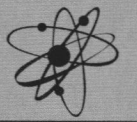

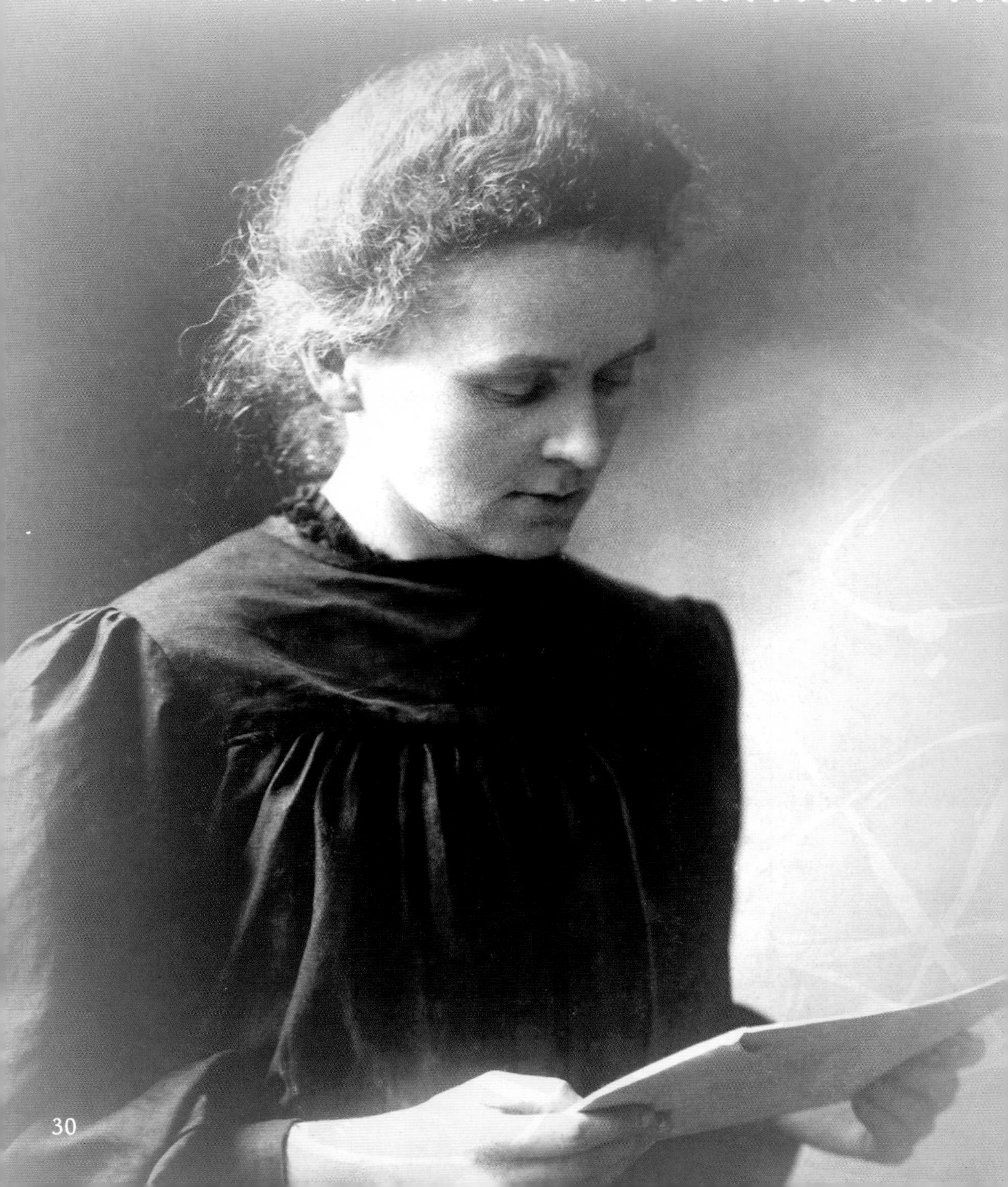

Name:	Maria Sklodowska Curie
Date of birth:	November 7, 1867
Nationality:	Polish
Birthplace:	Warsaw, Poland
Parents:	Wladyslaw and Bronisława Skłodowska
Husband:	Pierre Curie (1895–1906)
Children:	Irène Joliot-Curie (1897–1956) Ève Curie (1904–2007)
Date of death:	July 4, 1934
Place of burial:	Sancellemoz, France
Field of study:	Physics and chemistry
Known for:	Research in radioactivity and study of radium.
Contributions to Science:	Radiation research and the discovery of two new elements, radium and polonium
Awards and Honors:	Nobel Prize in physics, 1903; Nobel Prize in chemistry, 1911; first female professor at the Sorbonne

1867	Maria Sklodowska is born on November 7
1876	Maria's oldest sister dies from typhus
1878	Maria's mother dies of tuberculosis
1891	Enrolls at the Sorbonne in Paris, France; adopts the name "Marie"
1893	Finishes her master's degree in physics
1894	Finishes her master's degree in math
1895	Marries Pierre Curie, a physicist and science teacher; at Marie's urging, Pierre finishes his doctoral degree; begins studying radiation by separating and analyzing elements; German physicist Wilhelm Röntgen discovers X-rays
1896	Henri Becquerel discovers radioactivity
1897	The Curies' first child, Irène, is born
1898	Marie and Pierre study uranium and thorium and call the spontaneous decay "radioactivity"; they also discover two elements: polonium and radium; the Curies present their research at the first international physics conference in Paris

1900	Becomes the first female lecturer at a girls' school in Sèvres, a Paris suburb, and is the first instructor to include laboratory work with regular classes
1901	Wilhelm Röntgen becomes the first recipient of the Nobel Prize in physics
1903	Finishes her doctoral thesis; becomes the first woman to receive a doctorate in France; with Pierre, recieves the Nobel Prize in physics for their research in radiation; suffers a miscarriage
1904	The Curies' second child, Ève, is born; Pierre accepts a job teaching at the Sorbonne in Paris
1905	The Curies travel to Stockholm to give a Nobel Prize lecture on their work; Pierre is accepted in the French Academy of Sciences
1906	Pierre Curie is killed in an accident; Marie continues her radiation research on her own; becomes the first female professor at the Sorbonne; Lord Kelvin hypothesizes that radium is not an element, but rather a compound of lead and five helium atoms; Marie eventually produces a pure example of radium, proving that it is in fact an element

1909	The University of Paris and the Institut Pasteur build a laboratory for Marie, called the Radium Institute; in 1970, the Radium Institute and the Curie Foundation join forces to became the Institut Curie
1911	Receives the Nobel Prize in chemistry for her discovery of polonium and radium
1914	Works during World War I to provide X-ray machines for the treatment of wounded soldiers
1921	Travels to the United States to receive a gift of one gram of radium
1934	Dies of cancer on July 4 as a result of handling radioactive materials for many years

Glossary

atom—smallest particle of an element

atomic weight—combined weight of an atom's protons and neutrons

cancer—disease caused by cells that divide inappropriately

chemistry—branch of science that studies the structure of substances and how they combine and change under various conditions

curie unit—exact unit of measure for radiation

doctoral—advanced degree earned by study and research at a college or university

element—substance made of atoms with the same number of protons in their nuclei; cannot be broken down into simpler substances

gram—metric unit of mass

Nobel Prize—prize awarded each year for work in the fields of physics, chemistry, literature, physiology or medicine, and peace

physics—science of matter and energy and of interactions between the two

pitchblende—brownish-black mineral substance that is a source of a number of radioactive elements

polonium—radioactive element found in pitchblende

radiation—emission of energy waves

radioactive—being made up of atoms with nuclei that can break apart

radium—radioactive element

uranium—radioactive element found in pitchblende and used in nuclear power stations

Antoine Henri Becquerel (1852–1908)
French physicist who discovered radioactivity by accident in 1896 when a piece of uranium left in a dark desk drawer made an image on photographic plates

Niels Bohr (1885–1962)
Danish physicist who received the Nobel Prize in physics in 1922 for his contribution to understanding the structure of atoms that are made up of protons, neutrons, and electrons

James Chadwick (1891–1974)
British physicist who discovered the presence of neutrons in 1932; received the Nobel Prize in physics in 1935

Irène Joliot-Curie (1897–1956)
French chemist and daughter of Marie and Pierre Curie, who together with her husband received the Nobel Prize in chemistry in 1935 for the discovery of artificial radioactivity

John Dalton (1766–1844)
English chemist and physicist best known for developing the atomic theory

Albert Einstein (1879–1955)
German physicist best known for his theory of relativity and specifically mass-energy equivalence ($E = mc^2$)

Maria Goeppert-Mayer (1906–1972)
American physicist known for her research on the nucleus of an atom; received the Nobel Prize in physics in 1963, becoming the second woman to receive the award (Marie Curie was the first)

Dimitri Ivanovich Mendeleev (1834–1907)
Russian chemist credited with creating the first version of the periodic table of elements

Wilhelm Conrad Röntgen (1845–1923)
German physicist who discovered X-rays in 1895

Ernst Ruska (1906–1988)
Designed the first electron microscope in 1933; received the Nobel Prize in physics in 1986

Ernest Rutherford (1871–1937)
English physicist who studied the element uranium and became known as the "father of nuclear physics"

Joseph John Thomson (1856–1940)
English physicist known for the "plum pudding" model and the discoveries of the electron and isotopes; received the Nobel Prize in physics in 1906

Brallier, Jess M. *Who Was Albert Einstein?* New York: Grosset & Dunlap, 2002.

Fortey, Jacqueline. *Great Scientists.* London: DK, 2007.

Garcia, Kimberly. *Wilhelm Roentgen and the Discovery of X-Rays.* Bear, Del.: Mitchell Lane Publishers, 2003.

Pflaum, Rosalynd. *Marie Curie and Her Daughter Irene.* Minneapolis: Lerner Publications, 1993.

Tracy, Kathleen. *Pierre and Marie Curie and the Discovery of Radium.* Hockessin, Del.: Mitchell Lane Publishers, 2005.

Whiting, Jim. *John Dalton and the Atomic Theory.* Hockessin, Del.: Mitchell Lane Publishers, 2005.

On the Web

For more information on this topic, use FactHound.

1. Go to *www.facthound.com*

2. Type in this book ID: 0756539609

3. Click on the *Fetch It* button.

FactHound will find the best Web sites for you.

Index

Elizabeth R. Cregan

Elizabeth R. Cregan is a freelance writer living in Jamestown, Rhode Island. She enjoys writing about a wide variety of topics for children and young adults, including science, natural history, current events, and biography. She has bachelor of science in special education and a master's degree in distance education. She is also the owner of Cregan Associates, a consulting firm specializing in grant and technical writing for state government human services information technology clients.

Image Credits

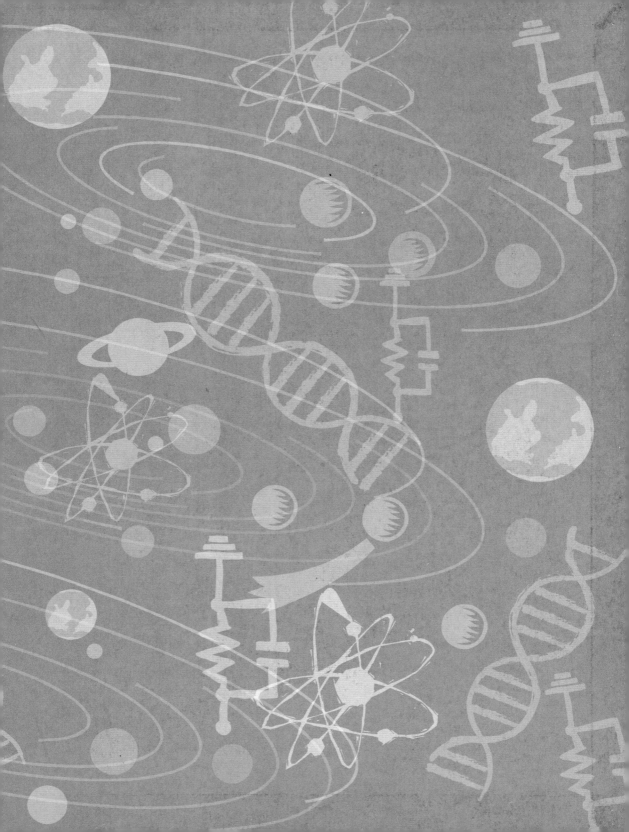